Meditations for Church School Teachers

Faithful Servant Series
Meditations for Church School Teachers

Nell E. Noonan
Christopher L. Webber, Series Editor

MOREHOUSE PUBLISHING
Harrisburg, Pennsylvania, USA

Anglican Book Centre
Toronto, Canada

Copyright © 2000 by Nell E. Noonan

Morehouse Publishing
P.O. Box 1321
Harrisburg, PA 17105

Anglican Book Centre
600 Jarvis Street
Toronto, Ontario, Canada M4Y2J6

Morehouse Publishing is a division of The Morehouse Group.

Unless otherwise noted, the Scripture quotations contained herein are from the New Revised Standard Version Bible, copyright © 1989 by the Division of Christian Education of the National Council of the Churches of Christ in the U.S.A. Used with permission. All rights reserved.

Printed in the United States of America
01 02 03 04 05   10 9 8 7 6 5 4 3 2

Cover design by Corey Kent

Library of Congress Cataloging-in-Publication Data

Noonan, Nell E.
Meditations for church school teachers / Nell E. Noonan
p. cm. — (Faithful servant series)
ISBN 0-8192-1861-8 (alk. paper)
1. Sunday school teachers—Prayer books and
devotions—English. I. Title. II. Series.
BV4596.S9 N66 2001
242'.69-dc21   00-060931

To my soul friend Emily Williams
whose encouragement to seek and to stretch
led me to this project

You Were Chosen

Were you chosen to read this book? Perhaps it was given to you in a public ceremony or maybe it was handed to you with a quiet "you might like to look at this." Maybe, on the other hand, it reached out to you in a bookstore and said, "Buy me!" Many books choose us in such ways and this book is likelier to have done so than most. But however this book came to you, it almost certainly happened because you have also been chosen for a ministry in the church or for church membership. Perhaps you hadn't considered this as being chosen; you thought you decided for yourself. But no, you were chosen. God acted first, and now you are where you are because God took that initiative.

God acts first—the Bible is very clear about that and God acts to choose us because God loves us. And who is this God who seeks us in so many ways, who calls us from our familiar and comfortable places and moves us into new parishes and new roles? Christians have been seeking answers to that question for a long time.

Part of the answer can be found within the church. We come to know God better by serving as church members and in church ministries. God is present with us and in others all around us as we worship and serve. But there is always more, and God never forces a way into our hearts. Rather, God waits for us to be quiet and open to a deeper relationship.

And that's what this book is about. This is not simply a book to read but to use, in the hope that you will set aside some time every day for prayer and the Bible—and for this book. So give yourself time not only to read but to consider, to think about, to meditate on what you have read. The writers of these short meditations have been where you are, thought about their experiences deeply, and come to know God better. Our prayer is that through their words and experiences and your reflection on them, you will continue to grow in knowledge and love—and faithful service—of this loving, seeking God.

— Christopher L. Webber
   Series Editor

Introduction

This collection of forty biblically based meditations was written specifically for church school teachers, those saints who have the audacious ministry of creating an environment where persons may come to know God and God's love story in new and profound ways. Their work is often challenging, frustrating, thankless, and difficult. It is also often humorous, joyous, exciting, and gratifying. However, no matter what the circumstances may be, church school teachers are engaged in mysterious, significant, and holy work. It is my fond hope that these meditations, based on experiences from my own teaching career, will encourage us to explore and to celebrate the sacred side of this important ministry.

— Nell Noonan

. . . in everything by prayer and supplication with thanksgiving let your requests be made known to God.

Philippians 4:6

Why didn't one of those religious education gurus or pundits tell me? I attended their instructional workshops and conferences. I read their books. But what I have learned on my own is that, even if I do nothing else as a church educator, I have to pray. When I make a commitment to teach, I accept a covenant responsibility with my Lord and my church family to touch minds and hearts and change lives. Surely, this holy work needs prayer—persistent and faith-filled, faithful prayer.

> Lord, you know that I truly find bliss in teaching now that I pray. I pray as I sit down to prepare, asking You to show me Your message and purpose for our session. I sense Your presence as I pray for my attendance list, calling each by name and picturing each child or adult with his or her own unique strengths, weaknesses, gifts, and concerns. Sometimes a child must return to an empty home after school, is adjusting to a new baby brother or a new stepparent, or has difficulty with learning

and socializing. Sometimes an adult is dealing with the loss of a spouse, job loss, serious health problems, or a crisis of faith. I commend each to You who knows his or her needs as no one else does. Lord, use me as a sensitive instrument of Your abiding love.

This is another of those occasions when I have waited until the night before a session to prepare. I pray to make the most of every precious minute of lesson prep time. But, even if I have to stay up until midnight, I will not shortchange time spent surrounding this ministry and the people it touches with prayer. I believe in its transformative energy and its mysterious power.

At the end of our class time, I perform a prayer ritual with the children that lends peace and reverence to what is traditionally chaotic dismissal time. Parents wait outside while we sign a blessing to one another. "Go now in peace; go now in peace. May the love of God surround you everywhere, everywhere you go."

Lord, surround those who teach with Your love. May this little book of meditations affirm and nurture them in their holy, life-giving ministry to Your honor and glory. Amen.

. . . so that you may lead lives worthy of the LORD, fully pleasing to him, as you bear fruit in every good work and as you grow in the knowledge of God.

Colossians 1:10

Some years ago I taught an adult class on the Psalms. One participant, a wonderful young man who taught at the university, was the father of three young boys. I called them the rainbow family because the oldest had brown hair and hazel eyes like the father, the middle boy was blonde and blue-eyed like the mother, and the third little guy was an adopted Vietnamese orphan named Michael.

After one session the father told me that he appreciated a Bible class where questions and "gut stuff" were allowed and welcomed. "This is REAL," he said. Suddenly the oldest son came up and began pulling his dad's hand. The eight-year-old said, "Something is wrong with Michael." We went scurrying to the Pre-K room. Michael was crying hysterically, flailing his arms about, shaking his head, and between sobs shouting "No, I can't go home, No, No, NO!" The mother made a bewildered gesture to the father. The two older brothers attempted to decipher a reason for this outburst and unusual behavior. Michael was always polite and well-behaved. This was very strange—very strange indeed.

invited to take one and place it at the table. When I light the candles, the *ahhhhs* are audible. We experience the Holy.

One day I walked into the classroom and found a little five-year-old on the floor with my story rug, the shepherd, and the sheep. Apparently her mother, also a teacher, had dropped her off early knowing I was away getting a cup of coffee and would be back shortly. I stood silently and listened. I heard her softly say, "I love you, Good Shepherd. Do you remember everyone's name?" As she brought a sheep forward, she said, "This is Jamie. This is Anna. This is Jeffrey . . ." She lovingly stroked their backs as she set them down. When she brought the last one forward, she leaned down to the Good Shepherd and whispered, "This one is ME, but you knew that already." I bowed the knees of my heart in reverence and awe. My soul rejoiced within me.

My Shepherd, King of Love, thank You for calling me to the joy of sharing You with others. May there be many more who hear You call their name.

*... we must grow up in every way into him who is the head,
into Christ, from whom the whole body,
joined and knit together ...*

Ephesians 4:15

Have you ever noticed how church school teachers slide into other volunteer jobs such as vacation church school? I recall one winter when that happened to me, but this call was not to teach. It was to be the director. Teacher recruitment was surprisingly easy. Curriculum decision-making was a piece of cake. The teachers loved the idea of using Marketplace 29 A.D., with learning centers spread about the church campus. Arrangements were made including an order to Mr. "Red" Bell for forty little handcrafted wooden crosses on neck cords. He had taken up woodworking upon his forced retirement after a serious heart attack and surgery. He could only work a few hours a day, but he was eager to furnish these gifts for our closing ceremony.

I was smug, thinking everything was going smoothly. Yep, piece of cake. The phone rang. It was the vicar saying, "Why don't we invite the Y summer camp kids to come to VCS?" I swallowed hard and, after a lengthy pause, asked, "How many kids are you talking about?" I hung up the phone a few minutes later with the shocked realization that our estimated forty children had grown to 128! We were a mission church with limited facilities but, more importantly, we were a church body with a generous heart. Men put up large canopy tents; women volunteered more snacks and supplies; contributions came in. The hardest part was calling Mr. Red because I knew he was in bad health, yet would push himself to make those additional eighty-eight crosses.

Over the decades I have experienced many generous hearts in my church families and have received unbelievable support. There have been woodcraftsmen named Canon Bush, Ed, George, Bob, Red, Jack, and Parks (who now makes the crosses). Artists, musicians, pray-ers, and many other parts of the body have worked together, sharing their gifts. Educational ministries would have been horribly diminished if not for saints like Donna, Sue, Jerree, Sandra, Henrietta, Dawn, and countless others far too numerous to mention. Yep, because of them, it's been a piece of cake and a blessing beyond measure.

Lord God, Source of love and generosity, thank You for those who have quietly promoted and provided for the building up of Your body in a spirit of love and comm-unity.

. . . but those who wait for the LORD shall renew their strength,
they shall mount up with wings like eagles . . .

Isaiah 40:31

The reasons I was exhausted in body, mind, and spirit were legion. I was suffering from burnout—physical, mental, and spiritual fatigue. There were days when I wanted to curl up on the mound of dirty laundry and go to sleep. Mothers of three young children who teach church school, lead a Scout group, work part-time at the library, and do myriad other odd jobs such as volunteer work, house-cleaning, yard work, and preparing three meals a day can find themselves in that condition—totally and unequivocally SPENT. Not only that, one of the children was scheduled for another eye surgery.

I was TIRED and unsure how I would keep going, but I read scripture and prayed. Just when I thought I would collapse, I was given a scholarship to a Christian Education conference at a retreat center in the North Carolina mountains My in-laws arranged for their wonderful housekeeper to care for the children. Feeling insecure and weary, with road map and directions in hand, I drove off.

I do not remember much about the workshops, the keynoter's words, worship services, food, or planned activities. I do remember a gentle, caring woman who was a perfect roommate and my companion for an afternoon hike to enjoy the mountain laurel in full bloom. I also remember a gradual awareness of a slow but steady renewal of body and spirit.

One morning we church educators gathered on a hillside overlooking the small, dark mountain lake. We were introduced to a song and the leader taught us motions to accompany the chorus: "And he will raise them up on eagle's wings, bear them on the breath of dawn, make them to shine like the sun, and hold them in the palm of his hand." At that moment I became happy and alive again. I often recount that experience and lead the song with the graceful motions when facilitating a church teacher session. Sometimes we suffer from burnout. We need each other and we need regular renewal.

What an amazing, awesome God You are! Thank You for reminders of Your steadfast presence that holds, renews, and refills.

He heals the brokenhearted, and binds up their wounds.

Psalm 147:3

I met her when she enrolled her daughter in the first communion course I taught on the four Saturday mornings during Advent. The parents were asked to attend the first hour of the first session, or any part of the sessions. Hannah (the name has been changed) was a single mom of beautiful seven-year-old Holly (name also changed).

There was a sadness about Hannah's eyes and a droop in her body language. She was quite pretty. After a brief dialog with her, I discerned that she was intelligent, talented, a devoted parent, and a caring Christian. Hannah was a fantastic quilter and she helped me with several banners and teaching aids over the next several months. We visited together as we worked and soon there was a rich friendship between us two women who knew something about being brokenhearted.

Many women and children all over the world have been treated in ways that maim and wound—physically, mentally, emotionally, spiritually. I do not mean to imply in any way whatsover that men, ethnic groups, religious groups, and others have been excluded from horrendous mistreatment and atrocities. Yet women, children, and the elderly are particularly vulnerable. Awareness of the staggering statistics of their abuse grows with each passing week. I knew the statistic that one in every three women has been sexually abused. I had read in a teacher's journal that teachers could figure that one in every four students was suffering from abuse. I thought about my beautiful young students. The horror and pain of it smothered me.

A couple of days before I moved to a new job in another state, Hannah brought me a farewell gift. The quilted wall hanging with its miniature pieces and intricate stitches hangs on my bedroom wall. What is not seen is the message written on the back: DEAR NELL, WHEN THIS YOU SEE—REMEMBER ME (AND HOLLY, TOO). It is signed and dated, and then Hannah added the version of the Lord's Prayer from the New Zealand Book of Common Prayer that I had shared with her: ETERNAL SPIRIT, EARTH-MAKER, PAIN-BEARER, LIFE-GIVER . . .

From the grip of all that is evil, free us, for You reign in the glory of the power that is Love, now and forever. Amen.

Beloved, let us love one another, because love is from God;
everyone who loves is born of God and knows God.

1 John 4:7

There is one in every class. I mean that child or adult (sometimes more than one) who challenges, stretches, and calls forth every ounce of self-control I can muster. She or he is disruptive, irritating, and a royal pain. Usually it is a little boy who creates such discomfort in my teaching ministry. I am not pointing fingers or casting aspersions here. After all, I am the mother and grandmother of some of those spirited, strong-willed, remarkable little people.

Being a grandma, I thought that I had mellowed out and that if I had one of those difficult children, I could handle it calmly and nonchalantly. Well, God chose to send a handsome little blonde boy to rattle that self-important confidence. This child simply could not be quiet. He talked incessantly. He poked the kids next to him. The thing that got to me most was his disrespect for others and his surly attitude when asked to obey our rules of courtesy and kindness. One morning he arrived early. I learned that his father and grandparents lived far away and that he was adjusting to life with a stepfather. I also learned that he was excited about his baptism in two weeks and I made a mental note to attend that service.

My student was calm, well-mannered, and quiet at his baptism. He was absorbing every word and gesture. He was given a baptismal taper lighted from the large Paschal candle. Suddenly he seemed all grown up. The light danced gracefully and joyfully on his peaceful countenance. His yellow hair, alive with the light, gave the appearance of an angel's halo.

This boy reminded me of another blonde boy in my kindergarten class about three decades earlier. I was exasperated with him on numerous occasions. One April Sunday morning he asked me in his husky little voice if I had taught Jesus when he was a little boy. I told him, "Oh, no, Jesus lived a long time ago and I am not that old." His prompt, serious comment was: "Poor Jesus, he never had you for his teacher."

Lord God, thank You for those holy moments that break into my ministry and remind me to persevere in love for all my students, even those who test me.

. . . as God said, "I will live in them and walk among them, and I will be their God, and they shall be my people . . ."

2 Corinthians 6:16

The unit was People of God, and the canned activities were dull. Even I would have labeled them BORING, so I could just imagine the response of my fourth and fifth graders. Something had to be done, but what? I was not sure they grasped the concept of people linked to one another, either historically or currently. They seemed indelibly shaped by the Western mind-set of individualism. They understood ME and MINE. I pondered how to instruct US and GOD'S. Will they understand covenantal relationship—the relationship that knows "You are my people and I am your God"? After all, the period of time covered in the Old and New Testaments stretches from around 2000 B.C. to A.D. 100. There seems to be so little in common with the postmodern world of my students.

I have no idea why I fretted beforehand. The children easily connected with the fears, ambitions, difficulties, problems, hopes, and surprises of the men, women, and children of the Bible. Our art project was a huge success. We made a tablecloth to be used at special church gatherings. It was like a quilt made from pieced-together squares and strips. The children were given muslin squares and fabric markers and told to make pictures of people of God. Later I pieced their pictures together with strips of blue and red calico. Large red appliquéd hearts were added to the corners. A permanent marker was used to write the date, the name of the church, and FROM THE FOURTH AND FIFTH GRADE CLASS on the hearts. Large calico letters saying PEOPLE OF GOD were ironed on the bottom edge using Stitch Witchery.

Predictably there were pictures of Moses with the tablets, Moses the baby, Miriam, Joseph in a colorful coat, Jesus, Mary and Joseph, Noah, the Twelve at table, and others. But there were also self-portraits, pictures of the priests, Mr. Ed the superintendent, parents, friends, and me. Separately each of us is a tiny, insignificant, frayed piece. United, each contributing the gift of itself, hemmed with prayer, we became bigger, stronger, more useful, transformed—a beautiful masterpiece.

Thank You, God of covenants, for choosing us to be Your people.

Let all the earth keep silence before him.

At the teacher workshop, I was introduced to signing. I learned that the sign for *father* was a thumb to the forehead meaning "head of the family" and "thinker." Then I was told that the sign for *mother* is a thumb to the chin meaning "talker." I resented that distinction until I began to think of the mother as storyteller, bearer of the faith stories, teacher of values and heritage, speaker of words of comfort and nurture. Her words might be words of scolding and gossip, but hopefully they are also words of kindness and instruction. Being mother, grandmother, teacher is a noble distinction.

I turned my attention back to the workshop and soon learned something I have taught hundreds of children (many adults, too) since that day. I learned to sign that wonderful favorite song of all generations, "Jesus Loves Me." The signs tug at my core, especially the sign for *Jesus* made by alternately touching the palms of the hands to signify the nail prints of our Lord. The sign for *loves* is to cross your arms over your chest and give yourself a little hug. The sign for *me* is simply pointing to your heart. I have discovered that one of the most powerful meditative prayers I can pray is to sign these three words, *Jesus loves me*, slowly,

Meditations for Church School Teachers – 17

repetitively, in silence. My soul becomes so profoundly engaged in communion, union, with my Lord and God that I experience a kind of spiritual homecoming.

That seems to be an experience shared with many others, far too young or far too sophisticated to express it, as together we sing and sign the song at the same time. Then we drop the music and words and make only the signs. I tell the children to let the signs go deep down into their heart rooms and never to forget them, never to forget God's love in Jesus.

Lord, I know that regardless of the changes, difficulties, brokenness, complexities, and confusions each of us will face in our lives, we will be okay if we remember "Jesus loves me." May it be so.

. . . so shall my word be that goes out from my mouth; it shall not return to me empty . . .

Isaiah 55:11

She was faithful—there every Sunday. She moved slowly (probably painfully), bent over a bit with osteoporosis; in her late seventies, I guessed. One morning she handed me a piece of paper and told me, "I used this when I taught Sunday School and thought you might like it." I thanked her, folded it, and stuck it in my purse. Days later when I found it, I discovered a recipe for a Bible Scripture Cake copied in beautiful but shaky penmanship. I immediately wondered, "Dare I take this class back into the kitchen after the sand candles?" My next thought was, "The children would love this. Besides, I simply cannot disappoint that dear lady. Have to do it."

Since the cake had to bake forty minutes and there was insufficient class time for that, I decided to make one on Saturday to take for the children to frost and eat. The class cake could bake during worship service and be ready for coffee hour. I got my Bible and the recipe and headed for my kitchen. Good thing I decided on that plan because I quickly learned that my Revised Standard Version did not work. I poured another cup of coffee and sat down deflated.

Some minutes later it occurred to me to look at the King James Version, the Bible of older generations. Puzzle solved!

I began. I creamed ½ cup Judges 5:25 (last clause) and 1½ tablespoons 1 Samuel 14:25 (second clause). I sifted 2 cups of 1 Kings 4:22 (first clause), ½ teaspoon Leviticus 2:13, 1 teaspoon Amos 4:5 (use modern powder), and 1 teaspoon 2 Chronicles 9:9. The next instruction was: "Add alternately with ½ cup of Judges 4:19 (second part) and follow Solomon's advice for making a good boy (Proverbs 23:14)." I proceeded through the remaining steps of the recipe.

On Sunday morning the children had a great time looking up the scriptures and cooking. Baking a sample ahead was a wonderful idea. Letting the children spread the chocolate icing, I turned from the sink of dirty dishes to see messy counters and happy children with smudges all over their faces and arms and Sunday finery.

Lord God, please help me find another way to teach my students about the nourishment found in Your scriptures.

Rejoice greatly, O daughter Zion! Shout aloud, O daughter Jerusalem! Lo, your king comes to you; triumphant and victorious is he, humble and riding on a donkey . . .

Zechariah 9:9

We are well into Lent now. Time to pull out that wonderful, intricate, wooden model of the city of Jerusalem and the little table painted to show the topography and where to place each piece. It is a great tool for learning about Jesus' entry into Jerusalem and the places and events of his Passion. I was scrambling that first time to get it ready to use. I probably was huffing, puffing, and mumbling audibly because suddenly an unsolicited volunteer from an unexpected source appeared to help me.

T. C. is the custodian, maintenance engineer, general handyman, and caretaker for every situation and possible physical need that could arise in the large church where I served as director of education and program. He helped me often with cleaning, repairing, moving, fixing, thinking about possibilities for improvement. We became good friends and I learned about his life experiences as a minority person. Our friendship has remained strong in the years long past my staff time at that church. At that Lenten time, however, I did not know that

T. C. liked to design and paint and was darned good at it. That big, strong former teacher did a super job. The only preparation remaining for Palm Sunday was to listen to an inspiring tape of Kathleen Battle singing a song that would be taught to the students: "O, what a beautiful city . . . Twelve gates into the city . . . O, what a beautiful city."

These gray Lenten days I think about Jerusalem, the Tower of Antonio, the home of Caiaphas, the three gates on each side of the city, the Pool of Siloam, the Mount of Olives. But mostly I think about the Via Dolorosa and the promise of peace, unity, and love that it brought to the world. I think about T. C. with the beautiful gold crucifix that he wears around his neck. I praise God that there will be NO prejudice or meanness or exclusion of anyone from the Great Banquet in the New Jerusalem. "O, what a beautiful city . . ."

All are precious in Your sight, Lord. May Your will be done on earth as it is in heaven.

I pray that the sharing of your faith may become effective when you perceive all the good that we may do for Christ.

Philemon 6

I was tired. I had moved. Everything about my life was changed. My husband made me promise that I would take a six-month sabbatical from church work. Yes, I was exhausted; I promised. Furthermore, my spiritual director was telling me the same thing. I adjusted to the change of pace easily. And then it began to happen. First, I joined a women's Bible study class and became a leader when the former leader moved. I decided to compile a Lenten booklet of forty meditations done by members of my new church family like I had done in other places I had lived. The next year I volunteered to teach a mini-series during Advent to first graders at the parish school.

The following year a teacher asked me why I had not come back and I told her that no one had asked me. Well, she asked and quickly arranged during Holy Week to have me teach all three first-grade classes. Like the previous teaching time, I loved being with the children again and telling them about God's love in Jesus Christ. I realized that that is where I find my bliss—with the children—but life was full of other things now. I was working on my Doctor of Ministry degree.

I was a Stephen Minister. I was teaching an adult class. "Forget the children," I told myself, "you are doing enough."

A few weeks later one of the teachers saw me at a church service and handed me a packet of letters from her students. As I read them I began to weep. These little ones were so hungry for the Good News and they were grateful that I had come to them. Their wonderful little drawings and expressive ways of communicating touched me deeply. Over and over again they said, "Thank you for telling me about God and Jesus." One question haunted me: "Will you come see us in second grade?" I promptly volunteered to design and teach a ten-week course on baptism and communion the next fall. I will continue as long as I am able. We simply must teach the children the faith stories.

Lord God, may we never be too tired to tell others the Good News of Your extravagant love.

‿

The earth is the LORD'S and all that is in it.

Psalm 24:1

I remember when I was in elementary school attending Miss Ellen Olsen's Sunday School class. One lesson was particularly unforgettable. She took us outside, and had us form a circle, drop hands, and then jump up and down. She marched us back into our classroom and proceeded to tell us that we had changed the world forever. She explained that our jumping up and down changed the earth for all time. We had packed the ground down. Seeds and roots and insects under our feet had been damaged or perhaps helped by our jumping. She continued and then concluded, "the earth will never be the same."

Miss Ellen told us that every single thing we do and say has consequences and that all of God's creation—people and nature—are affected. After the lesson, we sang, "Fairest Lord Jesus, ruler of all nature . . ." No one missed the point that Jesus cares about our choices and the way we live, that Creation and God's Son are connected to our behavior. God created everything. God gave us all that we are and have in this incredible universe. All is GIFT.

I do not remember Miss Ellen being moralistic about our choices. She never said that if we were bad or disrespectful stewards, we would be damned or sinful or whatever. She simply invited us to appreciate the wonder of sacredness and connectedness of Creator and created, gift and Giver. I have never forgotten my introduction to the theological concepts of interdependence and interconnectedness with the implied responsibility that accompanies those understandings. That dynamic, petite, white-haired spinster was a wise advocate and teacher of Creation theology with her simple lesson that sprang from a full heart. Her spirituality provided a natural model of thanks giving and thanks living that has had lasting influence on at least one of her impressionable young students.

O Divine Lord of Creation, thank you for special teachers whose spirituality provides bridges to the sacredness of all that is. May I be and do likewise.

". . . so that you and your children and your children's children may fear the LORD your God all the days of your life."

Deuteronomy 6:2

The six-year-old was walking restlessly about the entrance area of the church, climbing upon the retaining wall and walking across the top, going up and down the steps sliding his hand along the bannister. He was dressed in dark slacks and a crisp white short-sleeved shirt. His thick sandy hair caught the sunlight as he moved about quietly, aimlessly in his solitude. He seemed oblivious to the darkly garbed crowd as they streamed from their cars into the nave.

I met James when his grandmother (a colleague who shares my passion for Bible study) enrolled him in the communion course. He was so large and so mature for his age that I thought for months that he was a third-grader rather than a child just entering first grade. He was one of those delightful students who you intuitively know is engaged and happy in the learning experiences and environment you are providing. One day he had shared with us his concern for his great-grandfather who was dying. A beautiful little girl then told us about her grandfather who was also dying. Our prayers were soft, young, filling the room with a sweet fragrance.

I sat at the end of my pew remembering that holy time with the children. I thought about the generations of James's family. I stared at the huge, powerful Christus Rex that hangs from the high pitched ceiling of the sanctuary. It is a gift from this family. The rose window, also their gift, is high up on the wall just behind the altar. The community has gathered to honor the faithfulness and service of this dedicated churchman, a devout charter member of what has become a large, thriving congregation. James has quite a legacy.

As the family filed out behind the crucifer and the coffin and the clergy, James spotted me and beamed. He was happy to see his Sunday School teacher and he waved. I stuck out my hand and gave him a high five.

Mysterious Lord of Life and Death, may the generations be faithful in teaching Your mind-boggling Easter Story that love is beyond the touch of death.

"Just as I have loved you, you also should love one another."

John 13: 34

A colleague passed my open office door, stopped, and returned. She poked her head in and asked, "What are you doing?" I replied, "Making a yellow origami paper crane." When she asked why, I explained that I needed to know how long it took and how difficult it was. She shrugged her shoulders, raised an eyebrow, and walked away. Unlike most children, she never asked the next question: "Why do you want to know about making paper cranes?"

I did not get to explain about my lesson plan using the book *Sadako and a Thousand Cranes* by Elinor Coerr. I would have to wait until Sunday to explain about the Japanese tradition that proposes that anyone who folds one thousand paper cranes will have their deepest wish come true. Sadako Sasaki was two years old when the atomic bomb was dropped on her home city of Hiroshima. When she was nine she became ill and died as a result of radiation poisoning. She and her best friend began to fold the cranes as a prayer for health. Shortly before she died, she held up one of their 644 cranes and quietly said, "I will write peace on your wings and you will fly all over the world."

Sadako's classmates made the remaining cranes and placed them in a wreath over her body. With the help of their teacher, they began a fund campaign for a monument in Hiroshima Peace Park as a reminder of what the "Flash" had done to children. In 1958 a statue of Sadako was unveiled atop a large hollow pedestal of granite with a peace crane perched on her outstretched hand.

Peace—what is peace? How can I help my students get beneath the absence-of-war-and-conflict definition that tells little to nothing about what peace really is? Scripture reminds us that peace is solidly linked with justice. The two together call us to participate in transforming the world—in changing attitudes, behavior, structures, institutions, systems. Shalom is no less than the vision of God for the wholeness of our earth and of humankind.

Prince of Peace, in the words of that familiar song, "Let there be peace on earth, and let it begin with me" and my students.

And he took them up in his arms, laid his hands on them, and blessed them.

Mark 10:16

Two women came into the Wednesday morning Bible class and said, "We were talking about you at our Alpha meeting last night." I quickly asked, "Why was that?" They explained that there were some young parents present whose children had attended my ten-week communion course. The parents were impressed with how much their children learned. However, they seemed even more impressed with my firm discipline, and one technique in particular. When the little bell or silence did not work, I told some squirmy, chatting, neighbor-poking little boys that if they could not control themselves better, I simply had to conclude that they were still babies. "And do you know where babies who cannot take care of themselves sit? They sit on someone's lap. If you act like a baby, you must come sit on my lap and that would be embarrassing. I warn you not to push me because I have done it in the past and I will again if I have to." Any time a situation warranted, I simply would ask if the child wanted to come sit on my lap. The technique works great. Only one child in all the decades has pushed me into acting on my threat. My adult students, grandparents themselves, were immensely amused by my discipline style.

Lying in bed that night, I reflected on this scenario. I thought about when I get fidgety, talk too much, am out of harmony with my environment and others. Climbing into my Teacher's lap is necessary to regain inner peace. The Lord is always available and opens His arms when I approach. He pulls me into His lap, holds me so close that I feel the steady rhythm of His heart. My spirit quiets. I absorb His gifts of time, attention, grace, LOVE. He lays hands on me and anoints my head with oil. I fall asleep with a whisper of gratitude for His benediction.

Perhaps someday I will rethink my discipline style, but it works so well with young children that I will continue it for now. However, I will add one thing. When I pray for my students, I will picture each one being cuddled by our Lord.

Great Teacher, give us the wisdom to stop and climb into Your lap daily.

I sought the LORD, and he answered me, and delivered me from all my fears.

Psalm 34:4

They seemed so formidable. If the truth be known, I was afraid of them. I simply do not seem to connect well with high schoolers anymore. I did fine when my own three teenagers were around. I served on staff for youth weekends and loved every moment with those incredible, energetic, fantastic kids who never slept or hushed. However, the years changed me. This grandma likes her sleep and long periods of silence. Why, I puzzled, was I assigned to lead a group of high schoolers? I tried a few sessions and knew that this was not going to work well, but I showed up every Sunday. I prayed and I tried, but, with rare exception, the feelings of inadequacy remained.

One of those exceptions had to do with spoons—ordinary old soup spoons. We sat on old carpet surrounded by graffiti-covered walls amidst a hodgepodge of used, cast-off, mismatched sofas and chairs. Each person was given a spoon and told to hold it back-side up with the handle pointing toward his or her heart. They were instructed to look at what they saw on the back of the spoon. They quickly realized that their reflection was there. I asked them to go around the circle (with an option to pass) and tell about something that had gone right for them that week. I said I would go first and I told them about receiving photos of a grandchild. All eagerly participated, mentioning things like a good test score, a team victory, a driver's license, new shoes.

When asked to turn the spoons over and look again, they saw their reflections. But this time the images were inverted, wrong side up. Each was to tell about an upside-down thing in their lives. I told them about my father in the hospital and how much I wanted to be there. With the help of the spoons, these kids opened up. We learned about a cousin's suicide attempt, an uncle with terminal cancer, a sick dog, and other "wrong-side-up" things. As the spoons were placed on the floor in the shape of a cross, we made prayer requests. The experience was simple, powerful, connected, holy.

For Your presence in good times and in bad, we give You thanks, O Lord, our strength and our redeemer.

But let justice roll down like waters, and righteousness like an ever-flowing stream.

Amos 5:24

The dark eyes of a little boy hunkering down in mud near a tar-paper shack haunted me. His belly was distended and his arms and legs were so thin that the shape of his bones could be seen beneath taut skin. I thought, "How far removed we humans are from the theme of justice leaping from the pages of scripture. Can I somehow become a bridge between my affluent students and the world's hungry children?"

I decided to learn about hunger and ordered a *Hunger Action Handbook* advertised in *Seeds* magazine. One suggestion was to simulate the world food situation with a hunger meal. I mentioned the idea to my pastor. The next thing I knew I was in charge of staging this event the first Sunday in Lent for ALL classes combined! Why couldn't I keep my big mouth shut? I thought my purpose was to raise awareness so ten middle-school children could identify with hungry people. Now I was nervous and with good reason. Classes were invited to a special Lenten study but not told anything about it.

When the people arrived, they were given name tags with colored dots on them. One out of ten got a green dot. Three out of ten got blue dots. The remaining six got red dots. They were asked to get into groups of their color. The green group, representing the First World (Europe and the U.S.), were escorted to a table set with cloth, candles, flowers, real china. They were served a meal of meat, rice, gravy, broccoli, a roll, butter, apple pie, and a beverage of choice. They were told there was plenty more in the kitchen. The blue Second-World group (Eastern Bloc) were served rice, gravy, beans, and bread on simple pottery dishes. The 60 percent remaining, the Third World, were served a small portion of rice and water on cheap tin dishes. Oh, Lord, this is awful. The reactions! What a mess I'm in! Some are happy, some squirming, others angry. One fifth-grade boy is getting hostile: "THAT'S NOT FAIR. THAT'S NOT FAIR!"

Jesus, have mercy on me. My platter is too full and I don't know what to do.

. . . for I was hungry and you gave me food . . .

Matthew 25:35

I stood in the corner of the room watching the reactions to the hunger meal. My heart was thumping and breaking. I was as agitated as the Second-and Third-World participants. Then I noticed a fair-haired fourth-grader leave her bountiful table and take her apple pie and milk toward her five-year-old brother in the Third World group. She tapped him on the shoulder and silently extended it to him. He smiled and began to eat as she slipped quietly back to her seat.

The allotted time for the meal ran out and I rang the bell for everyone to gather for the most important part of the event—the discussion afterwards. How did they feel when they realized what their tag meant? How did they deal with the situation? How did they feel about their own group? How did they feel toward the other groups? What were ways in which they could have responded? How was this like the world food situation? How did it fall short?

The newsprint was filling up faster than I could write. There was high-energy participation from every single person there. And right on cue from the Holy Spirit, one adorable little boy asked, "What can we do for the hungry people?" The consensus was that we would pray and then come back the next week and discuss ideas on how we might get more involved with the problem of hunger.

That afternoon I was so exhausted that I took a long nap. "What can we do?" disturbed my sleep and my week. That question will always disturb me. The Bible does not give us a five-year plan or some great ten-step program for justice. Rather, the scriptures show us the Poor One among us who identified himself with the poor and hungry and those who suffer and are in need of help. The first Christians sought appropriate ways to imitate the Lord's own care and concern, to respond to the needy's cry for justice that was His cry. This Lent we, too, will respond to their cry, to His cry. That awful meal changed us.

Lord Jesus, may our caring and sharing make a difference for some of Your hungry children.

Save me, O God, for the waters have come up to my neck.

Psalm 69:1

Oh, you bet, God, I am praying and pleading for deliverance from the emotional and mental distress I am feeling right now. You see, I lost control. I lost control BIG TIME. I just cannot believe what I did. I don't even lose control often with my own children. I don't use bad language and I try always to be a lady. How could I lose control with a church school class of kids I hardly know? It just is so unlike me that I am in shock. But it happened, didn't it, Lord?

I was confident when I volunteered to teach the junior high class. I had taught children and adults. I was college educated and had attended numerous Christian Education workshops, conferences, and training events. I had a success record and was considered to be a skilled Christian educator. But I have been brought to my knees and I am hurting. This seems to be more than a blow to my perfectionistic ego. It feels like the *eschaton*, the end times, with earthquakes and cosmic convulsions, even though it is only my inner self that is being twisted and tormented.

I was so frustrated with those junior high kids. I had tried week after week to plan a good session. Sunday their smart mouths and disrespect for me, themselves, and one another spilled over into disrespect for you, God, to the point where they could not even repeat the Lord's Prayer together with some decency and honor. I felt the anger build and heat up. I banged by fists on the table and exploded, "DAMN IT, KIDS! YOU CAN'T EVEN SAY THE LORD'S PRAYER TOGETHER. I DON'T KNOW WHAT YOU WANT!" Tears came to my eyes. I left and sat outside on a garden bench. Later I phoned the priest and told him what happened. He said, "Don't quit; pray."

Lord, I don't know what those kids want and I don't know what You want. The waters have come up to my neck. Save me, O God.

But as for me, my prayer is to you, O LORD. At an acceptable time, O God, in the abundance of your steadfast love, answer me.

Psalm 69:13

I am doing as I was told. I am praying and turning this situation with the junior high kids over to God. I am listening. I feel a little movement within. I went back to the classroom the following Sunday. All twelve students showed up, too. I think they wanted to see what I would do next. I have returned every week and we are limping along with the curriculum.

I have begun to pray seriously for these "bad kids." I am trying to learn their stories, to look past their behavior, to see what is going on in their lives. It is crazy how the more I pray, the more I learn. The more I learn, the less bad they seem to be. One boy's father has stomach cancer. A girl is being raised by a grandmother who recently had a stroke. One student's parents are going through a messy and rather public divorce. The more I probe, the more I realize that only two of these kids come from stable, nurturing, normal family situations. The obnoxious behavior comes out of pain, confusion, bewilderment. Their bodies are changing. Everything is unsettled. When you add on the circumstances of their young lives, it is no surprise they act the way they do. Is there movement in me toward tolerance and compassion that was missing before?

We even did a good project together. I designed and made the picture of the Last Supper in the middle of a felt banner. The twelve students each chose a disciple and made a square with the traditional symbol for that disciple on it. Using a stencil they made the disciples' names and glued them beneath their squares, which formed an outer border for the meal scene.

But there is still no enthusiasm or vitality or joy of the Spirit. It gnaws at me that something is missing. In the recesses of my mind and heart, I hear the words reverberate over and over: "Don't quit; pray."

Lord, it is a miracle. I am learning to love these young people. In the abundance of Your time, show me how to teach and serve them so that they, too, may find their refuge in You.

Do not worry about anything, but in everything by prayer and supplication with thanksgiving let your requests be made known to God.

Philippians 4:6

I finally got the message. You simply cannot go about business as usual with this particular junior high class. I made my request: "Okay, God, in that case, WE better come up with another plan." I kept questioning what my prayer time told me. It seemed like such an unlikely answer. I was to teach the Church's Creed and the concept of the Trinity, but I was to do it by writing a script and having the students produce a marionette play.

Off I went to the city library. I discovered a wonderful resource on marionettes that even included stage construction and lighting. The script began to run around in my heart and mind. It began to dance. I felt infused with the Holy Spirit as the old dying man, twelve-year-old Peter, and Mrs. Jackson, the storekeeper, took on a life of their own. By the time the Christmas break was over, the script was ready. I presented the project to the class. The enthusiasm was *real!* The students decided to perform the play as a special event for the entire church family.

The three acts required three entirely different sets of scenery. The children learned about anatomical proportions and were quite studious and serious about the construction, stringing, and manipulation of the three marionettes. They built a cabin with front porch, a dock with fishing boat, and remarkable backdrops and lighting. Two absolutely perfect small, rustic rocking chairs turned up at a roadside market on a trip to the Great Smoky Mountains. I could not believe what was happening. The teamwork, the joy, and the sense of purpose and meaning were amazing. We were being transformed.

And then it happened. Two weeks before performance date, while their parents were in a Parents Without Partners meeting, some unsupervised children went into our classroom. We found the damaged marionettes stuffed down in boxes of old clothes in a back room where the women's bazaar supplies were stored. I felt stunned and twelve sets of eyes were watching me. My heart did not mean it, but I said, "I guess we'll just have to fix them."

Divine Miracle Worker and Mender of Souls, come and mend their broken handiwork and my broken heart.

God is love, and those who abide in love abide in God, and God abides in them.

1 John 4:16

My goodness, what a crucible this experience has been! It has, without a doubt, been the longest year of my church school teaching "career." The broken marionettes are patched, but are not the same. Peter has a chunk missing in the back of his head that I repaired and then covered with more sandy wool hair. Old Man "Sir" walks with a major limp because we never could get the knee joint wiring to go back as it was originally. Mrs. Jackson has a patched and repainted nose. The students have taken turns and have became quite skillful at manipulating the marionettes. They are a part of us now. There is a shiny new hinge lock at the top of the closet door to keep everything stored safely.

We met one Saturday morning with a church member from the university who helped us with an almost professional tape. The kids did a great job on the voices. We performed our own music which introduces and closes each act. "Joy Is Like the Rain" and "They'll Know We Are Christians by Our Love" are especially heartfelt and well done. The kids insisted that I sing one of the songs solo, with them humming a section. I have a passable voice but on tape the music is quite lovely. Everything is transformed on the tape. I am surprised at the excellent piece of work it is after editing.

Thanks to husband and a teenage son, a wonderful stage is constructed and wired with lighting. The backdrops are terrific, although wrought with much anguish on my part. All was proceeding well when one little cutie suddenly painted a blue streak down the handsome athlete's face and a paint war ensued. And there was the time when someone became amused while he had a mouth full of cola and sprayed everyone. And if you know seventh-grade boys, you know that burping was perpetual background noise. Then one of them would "break wind" and they would roll around on the floor laughing.

I am shocked to find how much I love these kids. At the same time I am miserable. When will this ever end?

God, I know You are about love and I know that I can't quit. But, please, Lord, my knees are getting calluses.

For the LORD is good; his steadfast love endures forever, and his faithfulness to all generations.

Psalm 100:5

I feel exhausted, spent, drained. At the same time I feel exhilarated, filled, energized. The marionette play is over! I sat in the back of the audience and let the students have full responsibility for EVERYTHING. I must have questioned my wisdom every ten minutes those last few days before the performance. But I stuck by my decision. They did it—not just well, but magnificently. I would put that performance up against the finest children's theater anywhere in the world. It was amazing what those gifted and remarkable kids did.

One of the mothers, a fabulous cook, organized an old-fashioned homemade ice cream social to follow the performance. There were overflowing platters of freshly baked cookies and churns of chocolate, vanilla, and peppermint ice cream. Ymmm!

The students had solicited businesses for little trinkets, notepads, and pencils, to which they added whistles and balloons. They enjoyed passing large baskets of these goodies among the audience. They had become fully excited about making this a special event for their church family.

We never did complete the curriculum designed to prepare students for confirmation. I may be inflating the importance of the experience for the kids, but I believe we learned about love, community, and church in ways that formed us deeply. We learned from our marionettes: Peter, representing Everyman, and Old Man Sir symbolizing the Trinity; God the Father—creating, loving; Christ the man—living and dying; and Holy Spirit—remaining with the boy and us after Sir's death.

I believe we grew to understand the play's title: "God Is a Verb, Not a Noun." Our experience showed me and, I hope, the kids that God is living, doing, transforming, and loving. At one point in the play, Old Man Sir says: *"En el principio era el Verbo, y el Verbo era con Dios, y el Verbo era Dios."* That's John 1:1 in Spanish and translated literally to English it means "In the beginning was the Verb, and the Verb was with God, and the Verb was God." In personal messages I wrote in books given to the kids at the end of the year, I thanked them for teaching me that God is a Verb.

Thank You, Verb. However, PLEASE send someone else to teach the junior highs.

Therefore we have been buried with him by baptism into death, so that, just as Christ was raised from the dead by the glory of the Father, so we too might walk in newness of life.

Romans 6:4

I have been accused of studying catalogs. I keep reminding my critics that even a merchant found a pearl of great value through his searchings. You never can tell what your seeking may uncover. The butterfly garden kit in the ABC School Supply catalog was one of those rare finds. I was planning Lent and Easter activities and what better tool for teaching about resurrection than its actual symbol in real live action. Without hesitation, I phoned 1-800-669-4222 and placed my order.

Two Sundays later the young students gathered around the table as I put together our bright pasteboard box with its large circular cellophane windows. I placed the flat petri dish full of chartreuse food gel on the floor and then I took the five caterpillars from their small dark box. In their new, light, airy environment, they began to uncurl and crawl about.

I carefully chose my comments that the larvae suggested the lowly condition of humankind on earth. A few days later their form was changed to seemingly lifeless chrysalises. These cocoons were attached precariously to the top of the box and hung there as if dead. Then one day to our delight the orange butterflies slowly emerged from their tombs like glorified bodies destined for eternal life. We dropped red sugar water on the cotton centers of the pasteboard flowers and watched these delightful creatures feed. All too soon the day came for taking them outdoors, blessing and then releasing them.

Back in our classroom, we reflected on our experience. Most let the butterflies go easily and happily. But Zack, my precocious five-year-old student, tugged at my heart when he matter-of-factly said those butterflies were going off to be angels with his father and Jesus. "I feel sad," he said. After a brief pause and shrugging one shoulder, he added, "I feel glad, too."

Thank you, Resurrected Lord, for your Easter people who somehow understand the mystery that there is victory even in death through You.

"I am the living bread that came down from heaven. Whoever eats of this bread will live forever; and the bread that I will give for the life of the world is my flesh."

John 6:51

The sound of the scraping, grinding, crushing, scrunching, groaning will not go away. It is the sound made by the grain mill built for our Bible Times unit. I was skeptical when I copied the diagram of a grinding mill from Nancy Williamson's *If You Lived in Bible Times*. No one will be able to do this, I thought to myself, but I took it to the planning meeting anyway. One young woman said, "Oh, sure, my husband can do that." And he did!

The grinding mill had one large, flat, round stepping stone (from the garden-supply store) on the bottom with a wooden axle sticking up from its center. Another flat stepping stone with a three-inch hole in the center and a wooden turning handle fit over the axle. Grain was poured in the hole a little at a time. When the top stone turned, the rubbing action of the two stones crushed and ground the grain into flour which fell from the mill onto a sheet. It actually worked! The children loved it. But the noise grated and irritated my comfort zone.

I wonder what it was like for our Lord that night alone in the olive garden. Did his prayer grind upon his spirit like a ponderous, heavy millstone? Was there a crushing, groaning noise as the stone slowly made its circuit? Turning, without beginning or end, pulverizing: "Thy will be done." Did blood sweat drops wrung from his brow indicate the cost of self-will leading to his obedience decision? Lord, how can it be that you are crushed into flour to be our Bread, to feed us who are always hungry? The gift—how enormous. I can scarce take it all in. Yet I feel a grinding of sorts on me and my spirit, too. Lord Jesus, you will have wrought one more heck of a miraculous, powerful miracle if you get flour from my willful will. But "All things are possible to the one who loves the Lord," and I do love You, Lord.

Give us this day our daily bread and crush us so that we, too, may become bread of life for the world.

On entering the house, they saw the child with Mary his mother;
and they knelt down and paid him homage. Then, opening their
treasure chests, they offered him gifts . . .

Matthew 2:11

In liturgical churches, the first feast in the new year is the Feast of the Epiphany celebrated on January 6 or the following Sunday. *Epiphany* means "manifestation" or "showing." Traditionally it is a celebration of the coming of the Magi to worship the Christ Child. The contrast between the rich, famous, educated, elegantly clad, big, powerful, gentile kings and the poor, humble, uneducated, swaddling-clothed, small, powerless, Jewish infant startles, shocks, surprises. O, how I love to tell this story.

The kindergarteners gathered around as I spread my white story rug on the floor. I took the large, chunky, preschool-style crèche figures out of a basket and put them into place as I retold the Incarnation story. I added the three kings to the scene and showed them three small velvet bags with their contents of ancient gold coins and samples of frankincense and myrrh. We sat there in silence and wonderment.

Some minutes later I asked, "If you could bring a gift to the Baby Jesus, what would you bring?" One little boy's hand immediately shot up in the air: "I know, I know." I asked, "David, that was quick. You didn't even have to think about your answer. What would you give the Baby Jesus?" "He doesn't want gold and that stuff. What he really wants is a puppy dog." I had no time to savor the wisdom before beautiful blonde Lindsay said, "I don't know what I would give him, but I know what I would do." "What is that, Lindsay?" She reached into the crèche scene and got the baby and gave that funny wooden figure a kiss.

I visited a nursing home. I read the story in Matthew to the two legally blind, depressed, dying women who share a room. I then asked them the question, "What would you bring Baby Jesus?" They became animated by the question just as the children had. It happened that one of the ladies was crocheting a baby afghan. When I suggested she make one for the Baby Jesus, she looked at me with dancing eyes and a beautiful, transforming, joy-filled smile.

Thank You, Lord, for the question and the blessing of epiphanies.

He has told you, O mortal, what is good; and what does the LORD require of you but to do justice, and to love kindness, and to walk humbly with your God?

Micah 6:8

I have been thinking about him a lot lately. He was such a *good* man and he meant so much to me and my sons. He treated me like a beloved daughter. I loved him and he loved me. When he died his three daughters insisted that I sit with them at his funeral. They even gave me one of the red roses from the arrangement on the top of his casket. It rests atop a bookcase in my office. I sense his presence.

You would never guess how we met. My family moved to a new town and a new church where I quickly became involved in teaching church school. That is just a part of who I am and what I do. I am a church school teacher. Besides, no matter where you go, there is a need for a church school teacher. "Mr. Ed" was the Sunday School superintendent. My adopted father was a retired postal worker who was God's own special ambassador.

Mr. Ed welcomed people, he got people connected, he took you to the coffee pot or drink machine. He gave every one of every age and every size and every status his time and attention. He would take up the collection and count noses and fix broken furniture. He would shrug his shoulders and tell you that he was just a little guy—not important, nothing to look at, getting old.

Yet he took roses from his garden to the hospitalized and homebound and us busy moms. He took young boys hunting and taught them how to make mocha. He organized the city's summer ball leagues. And he made sure that every kid he ever met knew that she or he was valued. He made wonderful wood crafts to share with anyone he thought might like them. Yes, a reliable, kind, loving, giving, simple man. I have known several saints, but the one that looms the largest in my heart will always be a Sunday School superintendent on his humble walk with God.

Lord God, bless all of Your church school teachers with their own "Mr. Ed" and warm memories of his or her very important ministry.

But when Jesus saw this, he . . . said to them, "Let the little children come to me; do not stop them; for it is to such as these that the kingdom of God belongs."

Mark 10:14

She was an exquisite little creature with dark shoulder-length ringlets, brown velvet eyes, and porcelain face. Her family had been invited by a neighbor family to attend our church. She entered the unfamiliar classroom of four- and five-year-olds without hesitation. She moved around the room touching and looking at everything, giving special attention to the large philodendron and a hand-carved wooden statue of the Good Shepherd with a lamb draped across his shoulders.

She was so very beautiful and yet there was something awkward and different about her movements. I could not put my finger on it and she haunted my thoughts. Her task each Sunday was to water the plant using a small white watering can. She seemed happiest while gently washing the leaves with damp cotton balls. When I rang the bell to call the children to the prayer table, the story rug, an art activity, or music, she did not come. I would have to go get her by the hand and lead her over. She never resisted but came willingly. After a time, I began to think that she might not be able to hear. On those rare occasion when she spoke, she was impossible to understand. She sounded like my friend who is deaf.

Six weeks went by and I decided to speak to the parents when they came to get her after class. I told them how much I enjoyed having her in our class. I also told them that I noticed that she did not seem to hear instructions. I had to be face-to-face in order for her to understand me. I asked if she had had a hearing test and suggested that, if not, they might want to have her tested. The father became quite agitated and told me in no uncertain terms that there was absolutely nothing wrong with his little girl. He stormed off and they never returned to our church. Soon afterward I moved out of state. I will never know what happened to the exquisitely beautiful little girl. She still haunts me.

O Lord, You love the little ones and so do I. Please, O please, watch over your child as her days increase. . . .

" . . . but God said, 'You shall not eat of the fruit of the tree that is in the middle of the garden . . .'"

It was a summertime intergenerational Sunday School experiment. Creation was the theme for June. The first Sunday we divided into seven small groups. Each was to make a symbol for their assigned day of creation, add it to a mobile hanging and tell their piece of the story. All was going well. We talked about some of our "favorite things God has made" and we sang "All things bright and beautiful." The plan was to close the session with Psalm 148: ". . . Young men and women alike, old and young together, Let them praise the name of the Lord. . . ."

Instead what came next was a powerful, gentle interruption. A highly intelligent, redheaded, eight-year-old boy raised his hand and asked this question: "If God wanted Adam and Eve to be good, why did he plant that tree in the garden?" I made my pat response: "That's a very good question, Chris. Very good question." The vicar began an explanation saying something about allegory, what the tree symbolized, and how people wanted to be like God. The boy started to frown and fidget. I interrupted, "May I please talk to Chris?" Turning to the child, I asked, "Why do YOU suppose God did something like that?" He quieted down.

Meditations for Church School Teachers – 59

It seemed like we could hear his silent pondering. A short time later he got a smile on his face, shrugged his shoulders, and said, "I don't know, but I'm going to think about it."

That was an exciting learning moment for me. Why do we need to have answers for the mysterious doings of God? Must we know why God does what God does? Why does God let bad things happen to good people? Why does God let good things happen to bad people? Why? Why? Like Jacob, Job, and Thomas, we struggle with our faith questions and their tentative, changing answers. Chris was asking a faith question; he was not seeking simple information. Chris's process was left open, but I began to squirm as I thought about students being closed down with hasty answers. How many have I unwittingly harmed in their growth toward a deeper faith?

Master Teacher, who taught by allowing individuals to struggle with their own personal process of faith, teach me to do the same.

Light is sweet, and it is pleasant for the eyes to see the sun.

Ecclesiastes 11:7

. . . and his face shone like the sun.

Matthew 17:2

We moved to the small university town where my husband was to begin graduate school. My three small children and I immediately liked our new church. I noticed an invitation (or should I say plea?) for church school teachers in the Sunday bulletin. I offered and was quickly led out of the nave into a dimly lit hallway to see my new classroom where third- and fourth-graders would convene in the fall. I took one look and felt a sense of gloom wash over me.

The room was small, painted white. The dirty white draperies hung down from the ends of the cheap rods like thin wet towels. The wooden bookcase was empty except for a small clutter of art supplies and old, faded teaching materials. The rectangular table and metal folding chairs were like those found in many old churches. Dull, uninviting, dismal was my assessment. I lamented about how we plan, budget, and fix our homes to be warm havens of comfort, hospitality, and beauty, yet, at the same time, many of our church homes are neglected. We pass the test when it comes to caring for spaces of worship, but the parish halls, classrooms, and libraries are often ignored, neglected, forgotten, or given low priority. I feel passionately that Christian Education is exciting business. Something had to be done about that unexciting environment.

My budget was as tight as that small congregation's was. What could I do? First I washed the walls, windows, baseboards, and door. I washed and ironed the curtains. I hung them to meet in the center and pulled them back with cheerful red calico tiebacks. For three weeks while the baby napped, every afternoon I worked on a 52" x 32" applique wall hanging of a glorious sunrise and rainbow fronted by rolling hills and a row of large red polka-dot tulips. I used calicos, gingham, and the brightest fabric scraps I could find in my sewing boxes. I covered cans and boxes with matching fabric to hold pencils and art supplies and added a lovely green plant to the bookcase. What a metamorphosis! Our space was bright, cheery, lively, full of sunlight, where the children and I would bask together in the Sonlight.

Shine, Jesus, shine; fill our hearts with Your love and Your glory.

Now to him who by the power at work within us is able to accomplish abundantly far more than all we can ask or imagine, to him be glory . . .

Ephesians 3:20–21

I cannot for the life of me understand it. Sunday School attendance is great at the beginning of the school year through Christmas but falls off in January. Life is hectic in the fall. When the pace slows and life settles into winter, you would think people would be better able to support their Sunday School program and would look for enriching activities. Hibernation simply does not make sense to me. After all, most Christian Education programs do that in the summer except for vacation church school.

I prayed for a "hook"—some way to keep my middlers attending during winter Sundays. I began a running dialog with the Lord. I heard, "Do a puppet play for the parish." I responded, "Good idea, but what shall we do?" The answer was simple, "Let the children decide." I sent postcards explaining the project. All fourteen students came that January Sunday. Nominations and voting led to their choice of Noah's Ark.

We worked feverishly for weeks on our papier mâché puppet heads and script. The children did good work deciding who and what they would be and say.

We learned to sing, "Rise and shine and give God your glory, glory." The children named themselves The 2 x 2 Company. They sent invitations to *everyone* they knew. The hand portions of the puppets were a joy to make as I prayed for each of my young puppeteers and tried to craft something that not only fit, but affirmed the value of their creations. I hit a stumbling block. There was one of those heads I did NOT like. One little boy made an ugly green ball with white smudged dots sitting atop a tubing neck. He said it was a frog. The others were so good but this one . . . An idea came: cut two balls from large white ball fringe and glue two small black fringe balls in the centers for eyes. I added legs with elbows akimbo and frog feet to a green felt body. That delightful, funny puppet photographed best of all the puppets sticking their heads out of portholes in our sixteen-foot pasteboard ark.

The cast and crew met in front of the ark to gustily lead the audience in "Rise and Shine" (all nine verses!) before making final bows. Rainbow sherbet, animal crackers, and rave reviews were dished out generously at the cast party.

Thank you, Lord God, for an incredible "hook" and a not-so-incredible frog to demonstrate again what the Holy Spirit can do for God's "glory, glory."

Then Jonah prayed to the LORD his God from the belly
of the fish, saying, "I called to the LORD out of my distress,
and he answered me."

Jonah 2:1–2

The spacious Sunday School room for four- and five-year-olds contained a children's worship area, a "prayer" area with a small table and cushions, tables and chairs, a puppet stage, bookcases with wonderful resources and art supplies, a lesson area, and a piano. The carpet was bright and cheerful. This was the perfect teaching environment—except for the dull, dingy white walls. One of my remedies was to make a felt wall hanging of Jonah in the whale's belly.

The art was simple—a side view of a gray whale cut in half to expose a pale pink "belly" where a small man dressed in blue extended his arms over his head. The water was dark blue with purple and aqua wavy accents and the sky was predictably pale blue. The plume of cascading water from the whale's blowhole, however, was not predictable. It took hours for me to cut and sew hundreds of small pieces of felt in shades of the colors of the rainbow beginning with indigo, light blue, purple, violet, greens, reds, orange, yellow, moving sequentially to white water droplets at the outer edge of the spray. The result was a delightful piece of folk art.

While I sewed, I watched the Olympics on television. One afternoon the programming was interrupted by a news bulletin. A plane had gone down at La Guardia. A couple of hours later I received a phone call. My cousin, who was a dear friend and talented young mother, and three of her children had been killed in the crash. The two-year-old had stayed behind at home with his father while the others visited "Grandmama."

The water droplets of the whale's blow became mingled with my tears as I sewed for hours, for weeks. Like Jonah, I cried out to the Lord in my distress. My heart ouches still when Jonah is mentioned.

Lord and Creator of us all, may we relish the moments we have with one another. And may the souls of the faithful departed rest in peace. Amen.

He said therefore, "What is the kingdom of God like? And to what should I compare it? It is like a mustard seed that someone took and sowed in the garden; it grew and became a tree, and the birds of the air made nests in its branches."

Luke 13:18–19

The children sat like "Indians" with crossed legs in a semicircle on the floor around the white story rug. I sat behind the rug facing them. I placed a 7" x 11" wooden "treasure chest" on the rug, opened the chest, took out a small oblong box, and opened it. We took turns looking at what was in the box. They were so tiny that they were barely perceptible. Someone guessed they were finely ground black pepper, which evoked another student's question, "Will they make me sneeze?"

Next I took tiny specks from the box and placed one on each child's extended finger. I explained to the children that these were real mustard seeds that came from the country where Jesus lived. I showed them a photograph of a young Israeli girl standing beside a large shrub. I asked, "Can you believe that big shrub grew out of a tiny seed like the one on your finger? Wonder how it got into that tiniest of seeds? How can something so tiny become something so big? What makes the seed grow?"

About this time I had to replace the seed Josh had lost from his finger. The wonder, however, could not be interrupted. "What does this tell us about the Kingdom of God? Is it in the highest and biggest? In the smallest and least? Does it look dead but is alive? Is it hidden but here? Are you like a seed? A growing, mysterious gift of life?"

I watched the children's faces and thought, "Yes, you are like the Kingdom of God. You are seeds, sacred signs of life. Present and presently here while at the same time you are hidden and becoming."

I am God's gardener chosen for this holy work. I am both excited and terrified— terrified until I remember the growth belongs to God.

Lord of All Life, watch over Your seeds and teach us the Easter secret of life that in giving up our lives to You, we live. Amen.

"Blessed are you when people revile you and persecute you . . . on my account."

Matthew 5:11

She is small of stature, with warm olive skin and dark hair that she twists and pins loosely in a knot on the top of her head. Her eyes are rich brown and when she smiles her cheeks get puffed and her face glows. She moves slowly with hobbled gait on feet and knees crippled by gout and arthritis. Barbara came alone from India to work on a master's degree in nursing at Boston College many years ago and stayed in America teaching, sharing, caring, blessing. When she attends worship services on Sunday and special occasions, she wears gorgeous saris and shawls—beautiful traditional Indian dress. When she approaches the altar to receive communion, she pulls a loose sari drape over her head in reverence and awe.

She rarely speaks up when study questions are discussed in the Wednesday morning women's Bible class that I have led for some years now, but when she does, we have learned, something important is being said. We were studying one of the Pauline letters. I asked, "Has any of you or someone you know been persecuted for the Gospel's sake?" Tears come to my eyes when I remember Barbara's description of her mother's treatment when she became a Christian and met ostracism and disownment by her family. She spoke softly about her own experiences. She told us about the tens of thousands who have fled their homeland and settled in our Texas metropolitan areas in recent years. She asked us to pray for those in India who are suffering martyrdom right now and for those Christians who were burned alive in their cars the very week I asked that question. She calls me her teacher and spiritual mentor. But we teachers know that Barbara and most of our students past and present are the real spiritual mentors. The Holy Spirit touches deeply and profoundly. My shallowness and glibness are pierced like a balloon. My heart takes off her shoes because I have found myself on holy ground.

Holy Spirit, Holy Mover of God, may I never forget the enormity of the gift of so many who have been persecuted because of their Christian faith. May I never forget the enormity of the gift I have of living in a nation founded on the principle of religious freedom. Amen.

. . . the angel said to them, ". . . to you is born this day in the city of David a Savior, who is the Messiah, the LORD."

Luke 2:10, 11

Advent is here. Boxes of Christmas decorations have been brought from the attic. The Advent wreath for the kitchen table and the crèche for the living room mantle always get unpacked first and are now settled in their "homes." I turn to a box marked "Angels" and begin taking each one from its tissue paper wrappings, placing them reverently on a small table. They come in an assortment of sizes and shapes. They are made of glass, wood, fabric, brass, wallpaper, raffia, plastic, crochet, pottery. Some are elaborate, some simple, some homemade, and some professionally crafted. But they have two things in common: each is an angel and each has a story.

The one I hold in my hand is two inches tall, white ceramic with hand-painted "sweet little girl" face. She wears a long white dress decorated with a border of tiny holly leaves. I recall the scene. I was teaching a Sunday School class of eight normal kindergartners and one little hellion. He sometimes hurt the other children and he made me dread our sessions. We often went out to the hall: "I love you, Matthew, but that kind of behavior is not allowed here."

Advent came and I realized Matthew quietly listened to the Nativity stories like the others. The week before Christmas, he handed me a tiny package that he obviously had wrapped himself with lots of Scotch tape. His mother explained, "He insisted on getting a gift for you and doing everything all by himself."

Thank you, dear God of angels and surprises; thank you.

The sea is his, for he made it, and the dry land, which his hands have formed. O come, let us worship and bow down, let us kneel before the LORD, our Maker!

Psalm 95:5–6

I love sea shells. Today I am looking over my recent acquisitions. I carefully place the sand dollars on a cookie sheet to go outside to dry and bleach in the sun. They will be used in a Sunday school session and given to the children. I recall the legend. The sand dollar has four nail holes and a larger one made by a Roman soldier's spear. One side has the imprint of an Easter lily with a star in its center to remind us of the star that appeared to the Wise Men and led them from afar. On the other side is etched the Christmas poinsettia. When broken open, five little white doves of peace and good will are released. The Love Story is here in this lowly shell. What an incredible gift to help me share the Good News with the children!

I look at other shells and anticipate what my students will be like. All will be gifts from our Maker like my gifts from the sea. Some will be fragile, delicate, easily broken, and must be handled gently. Each will have its own special beauty for me to discover. Some will have built a hard shell to protect themselves. I hold in my hand a shell that is chipped. No doubt I will have some students, young though they are, who have had difficult experiences that have chipped away a healthy self-image. Like these shells, they are in my hands now.

Come, Lord, and accompany me that I may teach in the pattern of Jesus.

One generation shall laud your works to another, and shall declare your mighty acts.

Psalm 145:4

I wonder how many times last Sunday morning I wanted to scream and pull my hair. I asked myself, Whatever in the world was I thinking when I came up with this idea? I had spent a tidy sum buying wax and wicking. I filled pots, pans, and pails with sand from the playground sandbox and lined them up neatly on the island in the church's kitchen. The twelve excited fifth-graders and I marched noisily to the kitchen, no doubt disturbing every class along the way. Each child got a container of sand to dampen and mold for a candle. Each was instructed to make three feet (like a three-legged stool), and shown how to fix a wick. Sand was everywhere. After I poured the melted wax, some ignored my warning and began to stick their fingers in it. They would peel off the wax and that too got everywhere. I was miserable but I managed to live through the smiles or scowls of the adults who came by to get coffee. Later I moved all the containers to the classroom and cleaned the kitchen. Wax on everything! DUMB, DUMB idea!

This Sunday morning the candles came out of their molds. We placed them on our classroom table. We trimmed the wicks and lit them. Each was so different and unique. No two alike. We talked about the transformation from liquid to solid to light-giving form. We talked about the people who walked in darkness until God sent the Light of Christ. Reflections of the light and Light danced in the children's eyes and moved about their wonder-filled faces.

Thank you, Lord of Light, for transformations and for the children who help me celebrate them.

She stood behind him at his feet, weeping, and began to bathe his feet with her tears and to dry them with her hair.

Luke 7:38

There were fourteen third and fourth graders who came surprisingly regularly to Sunday School that year. I had spent several hours one particular Saturday afternoon getting everything organized and rehearsed and "just so." Sunday morning came. We had our opening worship and were into the lesson when a little girl, who always chose to sit next to me, interrupted, "My grandmother said that a woman washed Jesus' feet with her tears and dried them with her hair. Is that true?" I thought to myself, "That's not the lesson that I have so carefully planned. What should I do, Lord?"

I stopped in midsentence and looked down into that little face with its disfiguring birthmark. I saw her inquiring heart and her need to know if it was "true." I paused for a long pregnant moment seeking some response. Then I said, "Yes, it is true. What kind of man do you suppose Jesus was to make her want to do something like that? Does anyone have any ideas about this Jesus who makes people do such things?" They began to wrestle with the questions. I never had to say another word as I listened to those wise children struggling to name the uniqueness and power of the Lord that affects the lives of all of us. We never did our lesson. We never did our activity. We never sang our closing song. But we did meet the Lord—the Lord who heals and loves—the Lord who heals a teacher with uptight lesson plans, a little girl with a birthmark, and a sinful woman of Jerusalem.

Thank you, Healer and Lover of souls.

Your word is a lamp to my feet and a light to my path.

Psalm 119:105

"I am the light of the world. Whoever follows me will never walk in darkness but will have the light of life."

John 8:12

It was an inspired idea—inviting the congregation to support us Christian education teachers through prayer and short-term gifts of their talents. One of the discoveries was a school art teacher named Jim. The theme for our unit was Everyday Life in Jesus' Day. Jim decided to help the students make small clay lamps.

I was mesmerized by his teaching style. He was quiet, gentle, relaxed, unrushed. Students welcomed his style and easily found places at tables covered with heavy plastic drop cloths. The tall, lanky man explained that small clay oil lamps were the source of light in the homes of early Palestine. The lamp sat on a simple stand or in a niche carved high in the wall so that its light could be seen by all in the house. He told us that when the family was away or asleep, an earthenware basket was placed over the flame so that it could burn safely while unattended. The people did not have matches and rekindling the flame was a chore. Because the flame was symbolic of the presence of God, it was kept burning even in the humblest homes.

With his sample lamp, Jim demonstrated how the lamps had a thin, rope-like wick and were fueled with olive oil. He told us some lamps had elaborate designs with several spouts and handles. Others were like his—a simple shallow dish, pinched at one end. While handing a four-inch ball of clay to each person, he explained what the psalmist was trying to tell us when he said that God's word is a light to our path. He spoke about Jesus being the light of the world and how we, too, can become the light of the world. Gracefully this man of faith led us through the steps of making a simple pinch pot lamp. Jim told us our lamps would be fired in the kiln, glazed, refired, blessed during the family worship service, and returned with wicking and small jars of oil the following Sunday.

Master Potter, may there always be oil in our lamps to keep us burning and sharing the Light.

About the Author

Nell is a passionate religious educator who has served in parish and diocesan educational ministry both as a volunteer and as a professional in many capacities for more than three decades. Nell's experience runs the gamut from volunteer classroom teacher to professional church staff as director of education and program to diocesan education minister for the Diocese of Mississippi. She holds a Master's degree in Religious Education and is presently working toward a Doctor of Ministry degree in Biblical Studies. She currently is a member of St. Alban's Episcopal Church, Arlington, Texas, where she teaches adults and children and is active in Stephen Ministry. Nell's family includes husband Bob, five married children, and twelve grandchildren.